Sauda

Zebunisa

And Other Poems

Sauda

Zebunisa
And Other Poems

ISBN/EAN: 9783744713023

Printed in Europe, USA, Canada, Australia, Japan

Cover: Foto ©Thomas Meinert / pixelio.de

More available books at **www.hansebooks.com**

ZEBŪNĪSA

AND

OTHER POEMS.

BY

SAUDA.

1873.

INDEX.

	PAGE
ZEBŪNĪSA	6
CLAIRE	16
UP IN THE HILLS	21
EVENING	18
MORNING	19
BOOT AND SADDLE	24
THE AMULET	25
LONGING	28
ANONYMA	31
LA BELLE CANADIENNE	33
THE SHELL GATHERERS	37

INDEX.

Fanny	39
Eveleen	42
Castles in the Air	55
Looking Back	58
Riddles	61
Spirit of Desire	63
Elléna	68
A Fragment	88
Au Revoir	92

ZEBŪNĪSA.

ZEBŪNĪSA.

FLUSH'D with the glow of Hindostan,
'T was evening, and with fiery span
O'er Shalabargh [1] the sun had cast
His crimson rays, and sunk at last.
And listlessly I lazy lay
Dreaming the weary hours away,
When suddenly my reverie
Was broken by a gentle sigh.

Zebūnīsa.

An Eastern beauty, young and fair,
All Houri-like, was standing there,
And tenderly she gazed on me,
Half lovingly, half bashfully.
She spoke—I strove to understand—
But, with a smile, she waved her hand,
And pointing to an aged crone,
She quietly loosed the silver zone [2]
That fondly clasped her slender waist,
And threw it to me—then, in haste,
She beckoned to her, and was gone,
Leaving me dazed, and all alone!

And there I lay, well pleased to be
The hero of such mystery,
For many an hour, until the stars
Shone softly through the tall chenars, [3]
And all around the fire-flies danced:
And still I lay there, half-entranced,
Yet listening to the faintest sound,
Impatiently I glanced around,
From time to time, in hope to see
Some messenger, expectantly.

Zebūnisa.

Nor vain the hope—the aged dame
At length with cautious foot-fall came,
The same that I had seen before,
A bundle in her arms she bore—
A boorgha,[4] and a spacious pair
Of silk pæjamas,[5] ladies wear,
With bangles,[6] jhangirs,[7] henna[8] too,
And broidered slippers, gold and blue.

She dressed me, staining hands and feet—
With looking-glass[9] and rings complete;
Then led me to the garden-gate,
Where patiently she bade me wait
A moment, while she went to bring
The Rūth,[10] and soon I heard the ring
And tinkle of its bells, that swung
Like fringe upon its purdahs strung.

She took me by the hand, and made
A sign to enter—I obeyed—
And getting in as best I could,
She followed me, and closed the hood.

Zebunīsa.

On silken cushions soft reclined,
To pleasure and my fate resigned,
I questioned her—but all in vain—
Discretion was her forte, 't was plain!
Her orders were the most precise—
She told me she had seen me twice,
Her mistress, often: but the *when*
And *where* she would not mention then.
Enough, that she intended me
To pass for a fair Kashmiri,[11]
(Wife of a rich Sheristadar),[12]
Who lived quite close to Shalimar,[13]
And sometimes came to spend the night
With her young mistress—very white,
And rather tall—so, if I'd bend
My knees a little, and attend
To her directions, all could be,
No doubt, conducted secretly.

And so we chatted—and we pass'd
The city gates,[14] and came at last
Before a mansion vast and high,
With figures painted curiously.[15]

Zebūnisa.

Then getting out, my wrinkled guide
Whispered: "Be careful, try to hide
"That which you are, as best you can:
"We're done for, if you're guess'd a man."

While thus she spoke, a little door [16]
Imbedded in the wall, the more
To screen it from men's prying gaze,
Was opened, and I saw a blaze
Of light within,—and by the glare
Perceived a servant standing there.

Forward with low salaam she came
To meet us, while the ancient dame:
"Go, warn our mistress that she may
"Receive the lady Dilrooba—[17]
"Her Greatness[18] follows." Then to me,
"Alight, your Highness, carefully—
"Permit your slave:" and then, aside,
"Be cautious—neighbours' eyes are wide." [13]
Passing within, she closed the door
Behind us, and I went before,

Zebūnisa.

Through a long passage, towards a flight
Of stairs, and with a step as light
As love could make it, half in dread
Of being discovered, up I sped.

Close followed by the crone, aghast,
Who panting,—whispered, "Not so fast,
"Such haste's against all etiquette,
"'Tis true there's little danger yet,
"You're *still* a lady; pray be cool,
"There's lots of time to play the fool
"'Tween this and morning, when you've met
"My mistress,—*pray*, Sir, don't forget
"We *may* have watchers, follow me,—
"It's *rash*,—I hate such levity."

And silently she led me through
A suite of rooms, where every hue
Seemed freshly stolen from summer skies,
Rich with the deepest rainbow dyes,
Where choicest Persian rugs were spread
All strewn with cushions—ruby-red,

Zebūnīsa.

Saffron, and pink, and that pale green,
That on the earliest leaves is seen—
And silver lamps their lustre shed
In rose-tint light, whilst overhead,
And all around, small mirrors[1] played
Like stars, as countless, myriad-rayed.

She paused; before us, white as milk,
A purdah swung, of damasque silk:
She gently raised it, and we passed
Beneath it,—and the die was cast!
For there, before me, beautiful,
(The sweetest still forbidden fruit is,)
Like a ripe peach for love to cull,
The loveliest,—Beauty[2] of the beauties,
Sweet Zebūnīsa, pensively
Stood waiting for us anxiously.
Her velvet cheek revealed the flush
Of expectation's fiery blush;
Her silvery[22] bosom rose and fell,
And *all* my love I longed to tell:
And raising her soft eyes she made
A little sign, that plainly said—

Zebūnisa.

"Advance" to *me*,—and "Leave us now,"
To the old dame,—who made a bow
With grave solemnity, and took
My boorgha off,—and then with look
Of mingled cunning and content,
Salaaming us, away she went.

I gazed on her, and she on me,
I loved her, and I felt that she
Returned it, and with usury.
Her glorious eyes o'erflowed on mine,
Rich crystals brimming full with wine;
Her eyebrows, as sharp Tulwars [23] curved,
Warned death, save velvet sheaths preserved.
While, like a cloud that folds the morn,
Her glittering doputah [24] was worn,
And thro' the fleecy silk there shone,
Throned o'er the midnight of her hair,
'Midst golden stars a golden sun, [25]
Studded with pearl and ruby rare.

White moteya-flowers, [26] lightly wreathed,
A cool, delicious fragrance breathed;

Zebūnisa.

An attar-dhan[27] of sandal too,
And pawn-dahn,[28] filled with spices, threw
Their rich perfumes' oppressiveness,
And, reeling with the sweet excess,
Soft on an amber silk resai[29]
Entranced we sank vuluptuously.

She struggled faintly, half denied,—
Then sighing turned her head aside;
I watched her swimming eyes, and caught
The secret of each longing thought,
Each amorous wish that wildly sped,
And wooed it ere it blushing fled—
With burning kisses—she replied
With answering kisses, and untied
Her ungeya[30] for my lips to rove
The globes of all a world of love.

CLAIRE.

HE moonbeams fell thro' the whispering leaves,
    Caressingly kissing each flowret fair;
'T was the mystical hour when fancy weaves
    Sweet spells of enchantment, richly rare.
'T was a night of voluptuous listlessness,
    When the fairest of faces we seem to see,
And I strove 'gainst the power of loveliness,
    Yet vainly strove, for I dreamed of thee.
'T was a dream of those darkly lustrous eyes,
    Of those tempting lips so ripely red;
And, methought, as I gazed o'er the starlit skies,
    That the past and the present paled and fled.

Claire.

'T was a dream of those darkly lustrous eyes,
    Of those tempting lips so ripely red;
And methought, as I gazed o'er the starlit skies,
    That the past and the present paled and fled.
And, yielding to fancy's powerful sway,
    I dreamt of the glorious olden time,
Of the golden customs of chivalry,
    When men *believed*, in their trust sublime.
And methought I knelt in a chapel fair,
    Where the organ pealed and the censers swung,
And by holy sisters assembled there
    In heavenly chorus the *Ave* was sung.
Softly and faintly the music stole,
    In lingering echoes it died away,
And I thought of the all-immortal soul,
    And the life I had led from day to day.
"Go forth, true Knight," love's whisper said,
    "Seek'st thou her love? o'er hill and dale
"Stay not to drink, nor court the shade,
    "While *right* shall suffer or *wrong* prevail.
"So let each deed of valour prove
    "Thy fame and honour as crystal clear;
"Be *true*, for truth is the *soul* of love;
    "Be *brave*:—thou hast but *God* to fear."

EVENING.

THE moon rose over the city,
    The sun sank into the sea,
There was music, and many a ditty
    Was sung to love's soft minstrelsy.

In my gondola gliding, half sadly
    She yielded to love and to me,
And *I loved her! yes;* recklessly, madly,
    Deliciously, dangerously.

As a star flashes downward from heaven,
    So memory flashes; yet we,
Being earthly, retain but the leaven
    That leavens love's infinity.

MORNING.

ASHED up by the sea,
    A pearl so rare,
Nothing to thee!
    Dead, and so fair.

Bright on her breast
    A cross of gold:
Passion's behest
    Who shall unfold?

Morning.

Snatched from her sleep,
    Life's loveliness,
Cast to the deep
    In her night-dress.

The cross of gold
    Is her burial fee;
'Her story told,
    Washed up by the Sea!

UP IN THE HILLS.

P to the hills, with a gallop-relay,
    From the sultry heat and the glare
Of the listless, wearisome Eastern day,
Where lightly we flirt the hours away,
Forgetting our duns, as best we may,
    With the Anglo-Indian fair.

Up in the hills, where the ladies tell
    Of the charms of a married life,

Up in the Hills.

As they whisper low to some youthful swell,
What a cruel hardship it is to dwell
Apart from the husband they love so well,
    When they act the loving wife.

Where you hang on a jânpân [31] and walk along
    By the side of your lovely one;
And you smile at the cuckoo's curious song,
As you wander by twilight the woods among,
Tho' of course you don't think of anything wrong,
    But it is *so lonely* alone.

And you get quite spooney, and half forget
    That your Leave is nearly over,
And with amorous warmth you're ready to bet
She's by far the prettiest woman you've met,
And for brooches and bracelets you run in debt,
    For they're fond of a generous lover.

And you look in her languishing hazel eyes,
    As many will do again;
And you long to believe her your own sweet prize,
And somehow you can't: but you don't despise,
For you know you can't love and still be wise,
    So strive to stifle the pain.

Up in the Hills.

With thrilling pressure your hand is prest,
    And maybe her lips you kiss :
But be it remembered, 'tis only in jest—
A pleasing excitement, with some little zest ;
I would'nt for worlds even hint at the rest,
    And *surely* there's nothing in this.

But the dreaded day at last arrives,
    And you part—perhaps for ever!
And you bid adieu to these model wives,
While your heart with reason for mastery strives,
And in truth or falsehood its tale contrives
    Of the *truth !* you're *sorry to sever!*

BOOT AND SADDLE.

OUR hearts were light, and we dreamed of pleasure,
Our arms were bright, and we dreamed of war,
Our lips seemed set to a joyous measure,
We bartered our kisses and gold at par.

Fair were the flowers of its sunlit maytime,
Glory and honor gleamed afar,
Gaily we rode thro' life's fresh spring-time,
Many a gallant bold Hussar.

Where are they *now ?* those careless faces;
Have they faded away with the dreams of youth?
They are changed, alas! and memory traces
But a dying gleam mid the lines of *truth*.

THE AMULET.

'T was many and many a mile away,
    In a far-off Eastern clime;
It was many and many a year ago,
    But memory laughs at time:

For it seems to me it was yesterday,
    And I can't get rid of the spell,
She came in the still pale moonlight,
    I remember vividly well.

The Amulet.

We met by a ruined temple
    In that far-off Eastern land,
And she led me away to her mistress,
    To the loveliest love of the band.

To the weariest bird of a dozen,
    The sweetest of Moslem ladies,
Along thro' the hushed Zénànà,
    Tho' love's approach forbade is.

Beneath the latticed windows,
    Where many a lascive one
Lay restless on a silken bed,
    Neglected and alone.

    *   *   *   *

The moon rode high in the heavens,
    And I cursed its glorious gleam,
Like a shower of gold to betray us,
    Till everything seemed a dream.

The stars like rubies glistened
    In a sea of sapphire set,
And the bulbul hymned as we listened,
    When she gave me this amulet.

The Amulet.

It is only a word in Persian,
    Engraved on an emerald square,
With a hole drilled through at one corner,
    But it hangs by a Houri's hair;
And the secret written upon it
    Is the simple secret—DARE!

LONGING.

SWEET the dreams that wandering fancy brings,
Soft whispering of the love we long to gain ;
And sweetly sad the wildly tearless pain
Of hope all hopeless, as its memory clings
With lingering love, and bears us back again
Midst well-remembered scenes, or softly sings,
With thoughtful music warbling the refrain
Of some light, loving love-song that we've heard
In other happier days, ere reason weighs a word.

Longing.

Sweet are the tender wishes that we feel,
Fair Idylls, bubbling up from hidden wells
Of purest loving ecstacy that swells
In noble natures toward the grand ideal
Of lovely woman's lovefulness, and tells
Of all the exhaustive struggle to conceal
An ardent temperament, where mind excels,
And hungering still for love, disdains to mate
With love of lesser range, though life pass desolate.

And sweet the bright foreshadowings of the hour,
When youthful ardor builds a glittering stair
Of golden resolutions, viewing there,
Queen over all, the lovely oné whose power,
Like angel counsel, leads us on to dare
The slippery, steep ascent, and cull tbe flower,
Life's choicest blossom, hanging in mid air
Of mingled passionate love and saintly fire,
Herself the blushing bud—*the all, a soul's desire.*

But sweeter, sweet the spell,—O sweeter far
The exquisite delirium that flows
In thrilling soft persuasiveness, and grows
Insensibly to fairest dreams, that are

Longing.

All but reality—as slumber throws
Its pitying veil o'er all the doubts that mar
Our waking vision, with fond passion's throes,
Of alternating hope and fear which dwell
Ever in truest hearts, that learn to love too well.

For O, 'tis slumbering thus we clasp the prize,
Draining love's quintessence of bliss, and cling
With maddening kisses to her lips, and wring
A wild consent from soft relenting eyes
And sigh-linked syllables, to everything—
To *all* our hopes of earthly paradise—
To wildest wishes—till the dream takes wing,
And waking suddenly, our fancy hails
Love's swift fulfilment near, as wavering hope prevails.

ANONYMA.

FOR the light of those eyes when the veined lids
 tremble and quiver,
Moist with the murder of sleep, all its sensuous
 exquisite pains;
Born of longings and lusts, as they surge and
and swell to the river,
The river that glides and glistens, glitters and gilds, and
 stains.
O! for the kiss-cut lips, blood-bathed with the blood of
 her lovers,

Anonyma.

Rich, and luscious, and red, the fountain of death and of life;
Robed in the mantle of gold, that sin's manifold multitude covers,
Seaméd and stitchéd with tears, *sans* girdle of maiden or wife.
O! for the weird wild thrill, the soul-sucked kisses of passion,
The rustle of silk and of starch, crushed close in the clutch of delight;
When the trembling fingers entwine, 'mid the temptress flounces of fashion,
When the loved one flushes and pales, and *burns* in her beautiful might.
Fill high, let us drink to our love—wine wrung from the vintage of pleasure—
See how it bubbles and brims, let us carry the cup while we may;
Let us mingle each pearl we possess, each jewel of price as a treasure,
For sufficient the evil of life, sufficient the debt to the day.

LA BELLE CANADIENNE.

'VE roamed o'er many a foreign clime,
   And sipped the glowing cup of pleasure,
And proved the folly many a time
   Of loving to repent at leisure.
I've seen the fairest English maids,
   With azure eyes and golden tresses,
And lingered midst the sunny glades,
   Where Italy the grape expresses.

La Belle Canadienne.

The lovely ones of Spain and France,
    Circassian, Russian, German ladies;
I've seen th' Egyptian Almes' dance,
    Cashmere, where many a beauteous maid is:
And mem'ry soon recalls the past,
    Each tender scene in groves Arcadian,
And wand'ring fancy's fixed at last,
    The loveliest maid's a fair Canadian.

You'll sail the world around nor find
    So sweet a theme for love's discussion,
United with a glowing mind,
    The charms of English, French and Russian:
And thus by walk and mien at first,
    Or by the tasteful way she dresses,
Is the feeling of admiration nurst,
    Till a magic power the heart confesses.

Enraptured with her easy grace,
    The poetry of every motion,
You raise your eyes to see her face,
    And fondly vow a life's devotion;

La Belle Canadienne.

While, swift as she returns the glance,
    Your senses reel in bliss Elysian,
She's the darkly liquid eyes of France,
    And seems to be a fair Parisian.

And when, in costly furs arrayed,
    She skims along the frozen waters,
Or softly whispers, not afraid,
    With silvery laugh of England's daughters,
As down the slippery cone you speed,
    Oh, *who* can paint the thrilling pleasure?
Whilst soldier-like you dare the deed,
    And boldly kiss your blushing treasure.

The graceful strength of Russian belles,
    Their pliant form and noble bearing,
Canadian loveliness excels,
    And well she loves a tale of daring.
Her throbbing bosom heaves, and then—
    With parted lips and melting glances
She pleads to hear it o'er again,
    In language that the *soul* entrances.

La Belle Canadienne.

So tho' I've travelled many a mile,
    And met with many charming beauties,
And fancied that I loved the while,
    Nor gave a thought to married duties;
There's only *one* I truly love,
    With purest love of style Amadian,*
And 'gainst a thousand Knights I'll prove,
    She's *loveliest* and a fair Canadian.

* Amadis de Gaul.

THE SHELL GATHERERS.

I STROLLED on the sands at sunset,
Away by the Western sea,
And I was aware of a stripling there
Gathering shells with a wistful care;
He picked them up and he washed them fair,
Then threw them away with a weary air,
And behold! he resembled me.

He seemed to seek some spell or power,
Some wondrous shell unknown:

The Shell Gatherers.

For they looked so bright, so pearly white,
They glittered and gleamed, and dazzled the sight,
Methought they were sure of the lad's delight;
But still with a sigh at the closing night,
He sought this only one.

I strolled again by those silver sands,
When moonlight kissed the wave,
And years had sped and hope had fled,
And life was unaccomplishéd,
I saw a weary man that led
The self same search; for *love* was dead,
And buried in the far-off Eastern lands.

FANNY.

HE passed me by as a duty,
With her soft eyes bent on the ground,
Yet she lingered near in her beauty,
Unconsciously probing the wound;
Perhaps she may not remember—
Perhaps 'twas a dream of mine;
'Twas Tuesday the 10th of December,
'Twas a dream amid music and wine.

Fanny.

I long to think she perceived me,
And sought but to rivet the chain:
That she doubted, yet wished to believe me
And I thought so again and again;
Her exquisite bosom seemed heaving
With fancies she strove to repress—
 And, passion its fairy tale weaving,
I'd have died for a single caress.

Alas! she may deem me conceited,
Nor pardon me telling my dream,
But think! by such memories heated
Can a lover refrain from the theme?
'Twas hope, like a beacon—flame lighted,
That gleamed o'er love's treacherous sea;
'Twas a haven of happiness sighted,
'Twas a vision of heaven to me.

How I hung on each sentence she uttered,
Translating its meaning and tone;
Like a school-girl's, my rebel heart fluttered—
I adored! and believed her my own.

Fanny.

'Twas a joy too ecstatic for reason,
So sweet! I perceived 'twas a sell—
'Twas love's wildest—love's last diapason,
Every note *now* re-echoes farewell.

EVELEEN.

ITHIN the fertile province of Tyrhoot,
Where the indigo-fields give richest fruit,
Where the air hangs faint with the mixt perfume
Of a myriad wond'rous flowers in bloom ;
Where the tiger lurks 'neath the palm-trees' shade
'Mid the jungle-grass where the deer have strayed,
Awaiting his prey — like a slighted fair
Cruelly calm, in his hidden lair ;

Eveleen.

In eighteen hundred and fifty-seven,
When the rebels had sworn by earth and heaven,
Not to leave a Feringhee[35] in Hindostan,
When the fiends were loose and thronged to the van,
And the vulture screeched with a warning cry,
And the crows cawed answer in revelry,
As they scented the carcases, black or white,
Foredoomed to their ravenous appetite:

With hot flushed cheek, and flashing eye,
A horseman wildly galloped by;
Both horse and man seemed sadly spent,
Both blood-besmeared,—yet on they went.
Sternly he rode some mile or so,
Swaying in faintness to and fro,
Then, reeling as with sudden wound,
Fell senseless, death-like to the ground;
Instant, the Arab checked his bound,
Sudden he reared and snapt the rein,—
Sniffed, pawed, and snorting, sniffed again;
A moment stood with listening ear,
Then headlong dashed away in fear,
Round and round in a mad career.

Eveleen.

Then, tired, with outstretched neck drew near
And sniffed once more,—his instinct knew
'Twas the sleep of life he slept:
Like a faithful servant, tried and true,
A weary watch he kept.
But he bit at the grass with famished bite,
And he neighed as tho' in pain ;
And he licked up the dew with a fierce delight,
Then shrilly neighed again.

And his master's eyelids quivered, and then
Slowly opened and closed again ;
For he dreamt of the morning's frenzied strife,
Of the hot pursuit, as he rode for life—
Cutting and slashing furiously
Thro' the rebel band that barred his way ;
And the moon rose calm and silvery,
And again he woke—but could it be ?
The thought was wildering ecstacy !
He strove to speak, but her finger-tips
Pressed lightly on his fevered lips :
He strove to rise, but all in vain,
He only fainted away with the pain,

Eveleen.

And there he lay, beneath the spell
Of eyes,—alas! remembered well,
Of gentle eyes that filled with tears
To find him thus,—unseen for years.
She dashed the diamond drops away
With one long sigh to memory,
And wistfully her satin hand
Clasped on his pulse, his features scanned—
She shuddered, and her looks revealed
Love answering love, till then concealed.
She'd nurse him with a sister's care,
Oh! could she leave him dying there?
And she called her servants and they made
A litter of shawls, and in it laid
They raised him gently,—a leaden load,
And bore him away to their lord's abode,
And they laid him on a silken bed,
They scarce knew whether alive or dead.
And the night-wind sighed 'mid the jasmine bowers,
And the bûlbûl hymned thro' the midnight hours,
And the golden light came over the hill,
And ever they found her, watching still.

* * * * * * *

Eveleen.

She nursed him, oh! so tenderly,
And nearly a month had glided by.
Nearly a month, and ne'er a kiss,
Nearly a month of torturing bliss,
They gazed into each other's eyes,
And wished and longed and yet were wise.
She tried to think of her absent lord—
And *thought*,—Is virtue its own reward?
She tried to think of her marriage-vow,
And so 'twas ever, then as now.

'Tis evening, and the stars look down
On the scorched-up grass, so short and brown.
They shine on the far-off hills of snow,
On the stately cedars, row in row,
On the groves of orange, and mangoe-trees,
Scarcely stirred by the sultry breeze:
They mirror themselves in the porphyry stone
Of a dainty dwelling that stands alone;
They gleam on its domes, where the gold once shone
On its massive pillars, with moss o'ergrown,
(It had served as a palace in ages gone,)

Eveleen.

And there, where the clustering garden-vines
Cast deepest shadow, a youth reclines,
And he gazes upward, but not to heaven,
To a daughter of earth his *soul* is given,
And he gazes long, and passionately,
And the daylight fades luxuriously;
He gazes till her lovely eyes
Grow wet with the love her vow denies.
And he rises from his flowery bed,
And her breath comes quick with a sudden dread,—
She knew it;—yet 'twas half unknown,
She loves,—and they are all alone.

* * * * * * *

Like a Houri, fresh from her love's caress,
She stood there in her loveliness;
Did she think of aught but her lover then?
She loved, and was adored again.
She had yielded; Oh! with a wild delight,
She had yielded all, in the dim twilight,
And her soft eyes swam with sensuousness,
And she dreamt of her sinful happiness.
Her velvet cheek, so flushed and pale,
Reflected passion's fiery trail;

Eveleen.

Her lips were wreathed with a conscious smile,
And his arm was round her waist the while:
He toyed with her long dark silky hair,
But he ate of the fruit such love must bear.

His wounds are healed, and honor calls,
He must join the force 'neath Delhi's walls.
He lingered, and oh! he longed to stay,
And the days like seconds sped away.
Each night he vowed should prove the last,
He dared not tell her—and it passed.

*   *   *   *   *   *   *
*   *   *   *   *   *   *

A horse stands saddled in the stall,
A sabre's clank rings thro' the hall:
He strains her fainting to his breast,
With all her passionate love confest,
And her tears fall fast as summer rain,—
They know they may never meet again.
And oh! the maddening agony,
The clinging kiss, the fond delay
Of eyes that swam beseechingly,
And wished, yet could not, would not stay.

Eveleen.

She had not loved him as she loved
Had she besought him unreproved;
She knew her power, nor spared the test,
He wavers,—mounts—she feels 'tis best.

But hark! that shout,—'tis borne afar,
It sighs on the wind with a wail of war,
Mingled with fiendish, vengeful yells,
Again, and yet again it swells.
Hark! 'tis the tomtom's[35] rallying sound:
Retreating rebels hover round.
Hark! to that yelp, for it rises near
In the broad daylight distinct and clear,—
'Tis the jackal's bark, and over the plain
They scurry in packs to the field of slain.
She listens,—can she feel no dread?
Are all her thoughts to terror dead?
She listens—'tis with thrilling joy—
He *cannot* leave her now alone,
Death only can their bliss destroy,
His honor and his love are one,
Now he is doubly all her own.

* * * * * * *
* * * * * * *

Eveleen.

There is a sound of revelry and din,
For Satan holds high carnival of sin;
Within the city walls the torches glare,
The zitars[34] ring, and tomtoms rend the air,
Whilst bhang[35] and noise and nautch girls [36] deaden dull despair.
Even the cold moon has risen redly rare,
Whitening the plain th' avenging ranks are seen;
Mark you that sentinel patrolling there?
Hear you the muttered curse his lips between?
See how he stops, and frowning counts the hair,[37]
And kisses reverently the tangled sheen,
Yet golden, as the moonrays intervene!
Oh! but the scenes thus conjured up are more
Than human heart can credit;—and the tear
Wrung from the war-worn soldier, as he treads
His weary watch, foretells the reckoning dear,
The doom decreed for many a mutineer!
Fast as the men fall-in, the whisper spreads,
And sword and bayonet reek with slaughter for Cawnpore.

List to the whirr, the hissing and the roar
Of shot and shell on deadly errand sent!

Eveleen.

Listen again—'tis answered by a snore,
Borne by the midnight breeze from yonder tent.
'Tis there the loving lord and lawful bore,
(And yet withal a very worthy man)
Fair Eveleen's husband, sleeps indifferent.
Look on his form! 'tis fashioned on the plan
Of some vast temple, but the god within
Is common wood; nor madd'ning love nor sin
Can change the block to godhead. He was one
(Their name is legion) only born to die,
For passion never signed the gift of life.
He liked her well—perhaps a trifle more
Than even his dinner; but the name of wife
Expressed to him no sweeter mystery.
'Twas not his fault; but then, alas! was she
Quite inexcusable, thus left alone,
Alone with love and opportunity?
He teased her, as such maudlin mortals can,
With kisses that are only half a kiss,
Then marvelled at the coldness of her mien.
Was she, love's loveliest rose to suffer this,
Nor scorn the drone that knew not how to steal
The secret honey from love's cave of bliss?

Eveleen.

Could she to such a one her *soul* reveal?
Our Saviour pardoned Mary Magdalene:
He pardoned her, *for she had loved much*.
Behold! the mysteries of love shall touch
The gold of Ophir seven times refined,
By exquisite pain and pleasure intertwined,
Till sin becometh virtue; and the mind,
Weaned from all selfishness shall compass things
Beyond the saints' most blest imaginings.
Pray for her soul, nor judge her hastily;
She sinned, she suffered, and her story brings,
This moral with love's wishful wanderings.

Shot by her lover's hand, lest she should be
Reserved for worse than death's swift agony—
Clasped by his circling arm, she drooped and fell:
Think you she gained the fields of Asphodel?
Lost in one last embrace, she died in bliss;
'Twas hard to die, but sweet to die like this.
She had lived too long, having tasted of the wine
Pressed from the grape of passion, all divine;
Ye would have dashed the poisoned cup away—
She drained it to the dregs in ecstasy—

Eveleen.

Doubtless she pays sweet pleasure's penalty.
And yet, perchance, in heaven was found a place
For yet another beauty in disgrace—
A *very* woman, with an angel's face.

      *   *   *   *   *

He mounted in haste and he leapt the wall :
In a last wild charge 'twere best to fall.
He could not endure the lingering fight
The assailants waged in their cowardly might.
Fiercely he rode, in bitterness—
The world was all a wilderness—
What cared he *now* for life or fame?
For *love ?*—'twere but an an empty name.
Madly he fought; with cut and thrust,
The astounded rebels bit the dust.
His sword swung red as the setting sun—
They deemed his life was a charmèd one;
Their bullets whizzed with a frantic aim,
At last the billeted bullet came.

They mangled the horse in their devilish whim,
They hacked his rider, limb from limb;
They fired the place, and the smoke was seen,

Eveleen.

For miles around,—through the air serene.
The flames shot upward, straight and strong,
The blackened ruins smouldered long ;
They looted and killed, but an ayah[32] fled
To a village near, so the story spread.

  * * * * *

The husband heard it, and vowed to kill
Both old and young for this deed of ill,
To spare in his wrath neither woman nor child :
'Twas thus he vowed in his fury wild.
But he knew not all ;—he was spared the sting.
As a drowning man to a straw will cling,
He believed her *true*, for he wished her so,
And the tale was vague—It is long ago.
He was buried in honour on Delhi's plain,
Around him a score of the rebel slain—
Their bones lie bleaching in sun and rain.

CASTLES IN THE AIR.

N the heyday of youth,
    When our thoughts are free of care;
    When life is all so rosy,
    Richly racy, debonair;
    Golden fancies sway the mind,
And we long to do and dare,
Whilst we dream of love and beauty,
      Building "Castles in the Air."

And when manhood sets its seal
On the careless and the gay,
'Tho' perchance we sigh for moments
That have lightly sped away;

Castles in the Air.

'Tis ambition rules us then,
With its fitful lurid glare,
And we puff our mild Havana,
    Building "Castles in the Air."

Tho' fondest hopes are blighted,
And misfortunes follow fast,
Tho' experience teaches lessons,
That we sadly learn at last;
Tho' we think that all is over,
Yet we never *quite* despair,
And we seek for consolation,
    Building "Castles in the Air."

For in this world of ours,
Were each lovely woman true,
Were every wish a certainty,
We'd look for nothing new;
And tho' reason says tis folly,
Yet 'tis bliss beyond compare,
And the wisest, best, and truest,
    Oft build "Castles in the Air."

Castles in the Air.

Let sages preach against it
In language calmly cold,
'Tis the old old story,
That's always being told;
We can scarcely take advice,
Tho' we're cheated everywhere,
Still we seek a fleeting pleasure,
      Building "Castles in the Air."

Yet when death is drawing near,
Let us dream of future bliss:
And its darkest terrors vanish,
For a fairer world than this
Softly opes its crystal portals,
While the silent power of prayer
Wafts our spirit to its Castles
      Everlasting in the Air.

LOOKING BACK.

OVER the earth, and over the sea,
My thoughts are flitting painfully,
Far and away beneath the spell
Of lustrous eyes remembered well;
And all around there seems to be
A nameless kind of minstrelsy—
Some whispered thought, but half expressed,
Or murmured longing unconfessed,
Dreams of what *was*, or *might have been*,
Dimly in memory's mirror seen;

Looking Back.

In all the glorious gleam of youth,
In all its ardor, hope, and truth,
Ere cold experience rules the mind,
Nor leaves but withering hearts behind;
Hearts that once loving, only see
A lifelong cursed satiety,
Whilst phantoms of the joyous past, ·
Silently, sadly, fleeting fast,
With icy fingers pointing show
The whirlwinds of the wind we sow.

   * * * *

Yet all is fair and beautiful,
 And the calm silence of the ·summer eve
Steals softly o'er each sense, and seems to lull
 The heart that lately, only throbbed to grieve,
Reminding that the sweetest hope we cull
 From beauty's glances, is but to believe
Each hidden charm perfection, and the rays
 Of swift intelligence from liquid eyes,
But sunny messengers of endless days—
 And nights of an exhaustless paradise
Of secret wishes, and as quick replies,
 Tho' not in words; but by the electric power

Looking Back.

Of mutual ecstasy; when soul meets soul,
    And winging heavenward, in a single hour,
Tastes purer joys than centuries can give
    To grosser natures; though the tempest lour
And years of undreamed agony may roll,
    Fierce on the track of pleasure; and we live
Th' ecstatic moments o'er, and realize
    Th' enthralling visions of the few who find
In that fair inner-world by fancy formed,
    A balm for disappointments, and despise
Those petty meannesses of humankind,
    Life's lukewarm Syrens, by no passion warmed,
Save calculating selfishness or lust
    That lured our boyish ardor; and the rust
And soilure of such loving wears away,
    Leaving but tempered steel, of truer, brighter ray.

RIDDLES.

WHAT is love? and what is glory?
    Are they nothing but a name?
Fitting subjects of a story,
    Ever endlessly the same.

Do we love, or love or peril
    For its pleasure or its gain?
Or some wild unreal ideal,
    That we seek on earth in vain?

Riddles.

Thus each care I strove to cancel,
    As I smoked my lone cigar,
Dreaming deep of dame and damsel,
    Loved and *left* in lands afar.

But the song my soul was singing,
    Sounded a funereal hymn,
Passion's belt of pearl unstringing,
    And my eyes with tears were dim;

Whispering softly, passing onward,
    Life's refrain, " *it might have been,*"
And remembrance travelled sunward,
    With the *ghost of youth* between.

THE SPIRIT OF DESIRE.

N a castle of the air,
Builded up with toil and care,
Lay the Spirit of Desire,
And his feet were shod with fire,
And his hands were filled with flowers,
Tokens from his paramours,
Tokens sweet of other time,
Lawless lust and love sublime,
Withered thoughts of every clime;

The Spirit of Desire.

Many a flower, rich and rare,
Bud and blossom, both were there.
Tied about with women's hair.

Came a lady unto him,
And her eyes with tears were dim,
And her voice fell very weak,
Very musical and meek ;
" O my darling, do your will,
" Be our love for good or ill ;
" I have prayed and I have wept,
" But my passion hath not slept ;
" I have striven to be good,
" I was e'er misunderstood ;
" I am sold for gold, and fee,
" 'Twas the price of my beauty,
" O my darling, pity me."

Then Desire answered her :
" O, my sweetest, I prefer,
" To the joys of the elect,
" That you lead me to expect.
" I have waited long to win :
" O, my sweetest, is it sin,

The Spirit of Desire.

"When love meeteth with his twin?
"It was ordered so above :
"Christ will pardon you your love :
"Is there any harm therein?"

Thus he whispered thro' the night,
As they revelled in delight;
So she made a pact with vice,
To exhaust each sweet caprice
Each delicious mode of strife,
Known to maiden or to wife,
Till he said : "Satiety
Is the curse that clings to me,
O beloved set me free."

    Sighing softly, she replied :
    "Can you bear to be denied,
    "Will you still believe me true,
    "Loving only, only you?
    "Am I not another's bride?
    "Yet you are not satisfied.
    "I am envied by the poor;
    "Did they know what I endure,
    "I would fain be cold and pure;

The Spirit of Desire.

"But alas! it may not be,
"For my breath is hot with bliss :
"I could kiss, and kiss, and kiss,
"There is nothing like to this.
"I have hungered for your love,
"And a snare about you wove,
"That you never more might rove."

Then the Spirit of Desire,
With his reason did enquire,
Loosed his shoes of burning fire.
And his visage all aflame,
Like a little child's became,
And he took another name ;
And his heart waxed very sore,
For the ill he wrought before,
And he vowed to rove no more.
    But alas, the lady fair
    Could not follow everywhere,
    Though she drew him by a hair.
Could not follow in the flight
Of his passion toward the light ;
Could not sail the wintry sea

The Spirit of Desire.

Of his soul's perplexity,
Of his life's adversity.
So he took his shoes again
From the place where they had lain,
And he girded up his heart
With an iron mask of art.
So he waits eternity,
All alone,—in slavery.

ELLÉNA.

OVER the mountains—far away
Where the Minal[39] gleam, and the Ibex[40] stray,
Over the snows where the lofty Pir[41]
Smiles o'er the valley of soft Kashmir.
Where lover-like, iciest torrents flow,
Impatient to woo the frail flowers below,
As plashing from rock to rock they toss,
Scattering foam on the velvet moss,
In pearls and diamonds, careless strewn
'Mid richest blocks of emerald stone.

Elléna.

Where the lotus⁽⁴²⁾ lilies sleep upon
The grave of many a lovely one,
Where the tall chenar⁽⁴³⁾ trees of fair Naseem⁽⁴⁴⁾
Have listened to many a tender dream,
Told by youthful lips and eyes,
Thinking earth was Paradise.

Many a dainty female slave,
And sweet Sultana, there reclining,
Has idly watched the rippling wave,
All tearfully her doom⁽⁴⁵⁾ divining.
Dove-eyed damosels, once enshrined
In the fairy towers so faintly seen,
'Midst waving bowers of jasmine twined
O'er the glittering isles that float between.

Dreamlike the ruined palace stands,
Light laughter sails on the passing wind,
And tiny feet on its golden sands
Their faint impressions leave behind.
Where the sim-badan⁽⁴⁶⁾ Kashmirian maids
Still throng the roses's⁽⁴⁷⁾ festival,
O lovely as the loveliest shades
That flit through the far-famed Peri Mahal.⁽⁴⁸⁾

Elléna.

* * * * * *
* * * * * *

And round our camp fire's ruddy light
We gathered, and with tale and jest
Sped far into the summer night,
Nor gave a thought to needful rest;
Tho' many a trophy strewed the ground,
Good proof our shots a billet found
In Markor,[49] Bear, or Barah-Singh,[50]
Or wild Chikor[51] of gorgeous wing.

T'was thus—we'd all the changes rung,
Some told a tale, and some had sung
A song of some sort,—all but one!
Our wildest one, and him we pressed
With laughing threats to tell us where,
So free of heart and debonair
He'd come by such a mournful air,
That now, when all so cheery shone
He held aloof, so quiet grown,
All silent, as a ghostly guest:
And looking up he seemed to smile,
But yet t'was half a frown the while,

Elléna.

And answering quickly,—" Are you then
" Such *boys*, as not to know that men
" Have hidden thoughts that seem to prey
" For *ever*, nor will wear away."
He turned,—we listening for a span
Bewildered,—as he thus began.

* * * * * *
* * * * * *

" In that sweet land, where love is worshipped still
Thro' every phantasy of good and ill,
Where still he reigns a *God*, indeed sublime,
The first-born darling of the bounteous clime;
Where lovers' philtres work a magic spell
And all is partly heaven and partly hell,
In sunny Spain, where wild romance can fling
Its secret charm o'er guilt's remorseful sting,
Where *yet* the amorous youth may take his fill
Of burning lust, to danger's madd'ning thrill,
And drain the essence of each earthly bliss,
Condensing all in love's long clinging kiss.

* * * * * *

In that soft land when Seville's vine
Blushed purple with its ruby wine,

Elléna.

When the orange gardens breathed perfume,
And the moonlight fell with glancing ray,
'Mid the fairest flowers of early bloom,
In glistening beams caressingly;
When I was young—and not as now
Of haggard look, and wrinkling brow.
And tho' long years have rolled away,
It seems to me but yesterday,
And still as even's single star
Shines sentinel, so lonely light
Fond passion thrills to hope afar,
Low whispering thro' the night,
And every breeze, that murmurs by,
Seems one long, soft, voluptuous sigh,
One of those lingering sighs that press
From the full heart, its tenderness,
And wishes, all to memory given,
Too sweet for earth, too wild for heaven,
Surge slowly past in wandering train,
Singing the old songs o'er again :

'Twas just that hour before the night
Steals upon sunset's amber-light,

Elléna.

When the vesper hymn ascends on high
In all devotion's ecstasy.
When mortal joys and hope divine
With mingling ardor half entwine,
And, borne away on fancy's wings,
We yield us to the dreams she brings.
 * * * * * *
And I lay by my window—wide for air—
And I felt that another day had gone,
But fate sat weaving a subtle snare
Swiftly, patiently, richly rare.
And sudden, silently standing there
I saw her—Seville's loveliest one,
Palely, sadly, sweetly fair,
One of those faces that we see,
And dream of to eternity,
Loving with love's intensity.
 * * * * * *
And I looked and longed, as we do in youth,
When our hearts are true and our vows are truth,
And I looked and loved, but I could not see
She had even a transient smile for me.
But she stood at her open lattice, and there
Leant over the sill with a thoughtful air,

Elléna.

Nor glanced to the right, nor glanced to the left,
But fixed on the pavement her soft eyes kept,
While her white hand toyed with the golden chain
Of a golden type of our Saviour's pain,
And it glistened and gleamed as it rose and fell
Storm-tossed, with her bosom's voluptuous swell.

And I ventured to strike a chord or two
Of one of the tenderest airs I knew,
And I practised many a loving wile,
Till at last she looked, yet never a smile.
But suddenly—leaving the chain alone
The soul of her queen-like beauty shone
Love-flusht in her eyes, as she raised them then
For a moment, and cast them down again
In deepest thought, and her color came
And went, with a flickering hectic flame,
Like fire in alabaster placed,
When its burning light is scarcely traced.

* * * * * *

But she closed the lattice, and still I stood,
And wondering mused on her pensive mood,

Elléna.

And the stars shone out o'er the silent town,
And the twilight faded, and night came down.
And the murmur of voices died away
In the darkening distance gradually;
And the moon rose slowly, and lightly streamed
On the tall Cathedral spires, that seemed
Like the burnished masts of beaten gold
Of ships in the Eastern fables old,
And the fleecy clouds were the silken sails
Unfurled to the breath of its perfumed gales.

And the street seemed deserted—only one,
A man in a cloak came by, alone,
In a long dark cloak, such as lovers wear
When they steal by night to some lady fair:
And I heeded him not till I saw him take
A key from his pocket, and swiftly make
For the opposite mansion, and cast a look
Down the silent street—then I also took
A wondering glance, and perceived a door
In the garden wall, unseen before,
And he opened it quickly and turned the key,
As he closed it after him noiselessly.

Elléna.

* * * * * *
* * * * * *

I glanced at a clock in a Convent tower
Lit by a moonbeam's passing ray,
I wearily watched the light clouds lour
Over the mansion lingeringly,
Thinking on all this mystery:
And an hour or so had slipped away,
I wondering still, when cautiously
A blind was raised—with anxious eye
I watched it,—all in dreamy lull
Slept silent, calm, and beautiful.
Not another sound to break the spell
Save the dreary toll of the Convent bell,
Swinging so high in the belfry there,
To and fro in the sultry air.
* * * * * *
But the moon shines out, and I soon descry
That a lady leans on the balcony
'Tis she, my lovely pale unknown,
Paler than ever, and all alone.
And she fixes her large dark eyes on mine,
Not bashfully now, but in calm design,

Elléna.

As if she would read my thoughts, and test
To the uttermost all my looks exprest:
And I hazard a sign, and think I see
A wavering smile flit over her lips,
And another sign is returned to me,
For she closes them quick with her finger-tips,
As she holds up a tiny note, and a key,
And in half a second I stand beneath
The balcony, waiting with bated breath,
And I catch the note and key as they fall
And fly to my room, but first in the hall
Tear open the note, and read these words
In French, by the glimmer the lamp affords:
" Are you discreet and brave, and can
" I trust you wholly?"—thus it ran,
" Can I believe you?—Yes, I will
" Come then to-night, when all is still,
" Enter the garden door, this key
" Will open it, and there wait for me;
" The greatest caution, avoid the light—
" I'll come, don't venture ere midnight."

  * * * * * *
  * * * * * *

Elléna.

I kissed the note a hundred times and more,
I covered it with kisses, for I thought,
Although the blind was lowered as before,
Most probably she watched me, and I caught
The glitter of a hand that waved a sign
To show that she expected me, and then
Hope gave a loose to lovefulness,—"She's mine,"
Was joy unutterably sweet, as when
Some tempting prize we wish, but hardly dare
Even to hope to win with weary toil,
Drops from the clouds—love's manna from the air—
Or like the mangoe seed in gen'rous soil,
When quickly ripened by the Juggler's art,
It springs up suddenly, and, if a cheat,
Appears of nature's handiwork a part,
Nor seems unreal to us, for if we eat
The blushing fruit is luscious to the taste,
Sweet as the sweetest plucked, tho' grown in magic haste.

*   *   *   *   *   *

And so forgetting everything but this,
And only thinking how t'were best to pass
The intervening hours away, nor miss
A chance of pleasing her, before the glass,
With careful carelessness and many a sigh

Elléna.

That rose impatiently, I dressed again
With trembling fingers that put all awry,
So that I scarce from thinking could refrain
That all was but a dream, till chimed the hour
The wished twelve bell-notes, ringing from the tower
In sweetest warning, and I quickly caught
My pistols up, and gained the little door
And gently opened it, and waiting sought
To pierce the darkness, where the clust'ring vine
Grew thickest, till a hand was placed in mine,
A soft warm hand, that shot a fevered thrill
Of mad'ning happiness, so wild t'would kill
Did it exceed a second, and I heard
The rustling of a dress, but not a word
Was spoken,—and she hurried on, before,
And, following a long corridor, we came
Beneath a staircase of dark polished wood,
With gilded bannisters, and many a dame
And noble knight in pictured life-length stood
Along the wall,—while marble statues gleamed
Like ghosts upon each landing place, and seemed
To bar the passage, and she led the way
Up the wide stair, to where a feeble ray

Elléna.

Just glimmering thro' a doorway cast a light,
Pale struggling with the moonbeams, where the night
Appeared to gather darkest, and we turned
And passed the threshold, and I found myself
In a large room, where two tall candles burned :
And on its panels of dark ebony
Were silver shields, and on them graved the arms
And all devices of the family,
Together with some wond'rous olden charms
To scare away the devil, or each elf
Of wickedness that dared to enter it.
But only partially the room was lit,
And at one end a massive bedstead stood,
With satin curtains closed on every side.
And here she loitered, as in thoughtful mood
With secret sorrow, blushingly denied;
While, flusht with rapture, I detained her hand,
Kissing it fast—Oh could I but forget !—
Kneeling in adoration, and her grand
Mysterious mournful eyes, all lustre-wet,
Mirrored on mine and questioned them for love.
  * * * * * *
And thus I told the olden story o'er,
And only asked a way its truth to prove,

Elléna.

To show her that her lightest wish was more,
Far more to me than life or wealth or fame.
And bending low she whispered, "Will you blame
My doubting you? You swear it?" And I swore,
Swore by the little crucifix she wore,
To do whatever she should ask of me.
Then lowering closer still her queenly head
And murmuring, "You're a noble cavalier,
All, all, I hoped," she rose, and toward the bed
She led me hastily,—but still the fear
That all was but some dreamy phantasy
Harassed my senses, and quite drunk with love,
And hungering for reality, I strove
To draw the curtains open, but her hand,
Nerved with excitement, careless of command,
Midway arrested mine, and with a look,
A look of speechless agony, that shook
All power of reasoning, she gazed on me.
And straining her with passion to my breast,
I kissed with clinging kisses that confest
My frenzied love, and urged her not to be
Thus frightened, but to tell me all her fears,
And asked her why she trembled, but her tears

Elléna.

Were all her answer, and she clung to me.
  * * * * * *
  * * * * * *
I tore the curtains hurriedly aside :
A gay dragoon lay prone extended there,
Quite motionless,—a youth, in all the pride
Of early manhood,—and his face, as fair
And smooth to look upon as any girl's,
Gleamed ghastly in the moonlight, while his curls
Streaked the white pillow-case with lines of blood,
In crimson streamlets coursing silently.
But still the expression of his features showed
The trace of pleasure, joyed in recently,
Telling he met his cruel fate, when all
His feelings warred against it, and the thrall
And darkening doom of death were quite forgot.
A sickening horror chained me to the spot,
And, while I gazed, my voice refused to sound
Save in a hoarse low whisper, murmuring on,
" What have you done ? My God ! What have you done ?"
  * * * * * *

Slowly, but solemnly, she answered me :
" I did but justice ! stay,—a single word

Elléna.

"Will justify me, tho' 'tis death to me—
" He proved unfaithful. 'Tis the one award
" Of treachery,--be warned by it, nor dare
" Though loved with tend'rest love, betray the trust
" Of Andalusia's daughters: for *we* spare
" No sacrifice, but love with passion's gust,
"With *all* our fiery nature loosed to win
" Your hearts and souls, regardless of the sin:
" And tho' we die of grief, as I shall die
" For having done this deed, through very love,
" 'Twere better so, than feel love's agony,
" Th' excruciating torture-coils that wove
" All snake-like round my heart. 'Twas jealousy,
" And oh! though you may hate me, yet you swore,
" Swore by the holy cross, to venture all
" To do me service, and to think no more
" Of fame or life or duty at the call,
" Vowing you *longed* to prove it; think of this,
" Think *how* you swore it,—for a single kiss.
" O take away the corpse, *take it away!*
" I cannot, dare not look upon him thus:
" I loved him,—O how fondly none can say,
" Except my cruel self, and, credulous

Elléna.

"With woman's ardor, I believed him true.
"Oh! is not this *my punishment?*—and you,
"Will you not help me?" And her deep despair
But made her look the lovelier; I'd have dared
A thousand deaths to save her, and to bear
The fearful burden forth I stood prepared,
While, with extremity of danger calm,
"Madam, you ask my life," I said, "'tis yours."
"O now," she cried, "I love you,—*yes*, the balm
"Of such unreasoning passion half restores
"My faith in man; I love you, and yet *now*
"Am all unworthy of your love; O how,
"How can I now reward you?" And she knelt
All tearfully before me, and I felt
The spell of loveliness in all its force,
And raised her up and kissed her, while remorse,
Delight, and horror mingled in my mind.
But passion quickly triumphed, and I twined
My arms about her, whispering, "Be brave!
"Have I not sworn it? I am *still* your slave:
"Away with tears, and let us act, nor waste
"A moment more;" and lifting up in haste
And staggering 'neath the corpse, I gained the door,

Elléna.

But, catching sight of something on the floor,
She pointed to it, and it proved a cloak—
She flung it o'er the body. But I woke
To even greater horror—'twas the same,
The self-same brown one of the man who came
That very night, and entered by the key,
Perchance the very key she gave to me.
Then, seeing all love's struggle on my face,
And touched with tenderness, she tried to trace
The danger I was running for her, " Stay,
" O fly while yet there's time to fly : away,
" Nor think of me at all," she wildly cried,
" You're lost if you are met ; 'twere vain to hide
" The fatal truth ;" " And you then ?" I replied,
" Are *you* not lost if this remains till day?
" Already I perceive the dawning grey,
" The tell-tale lights of morning, and you say
" Fly while there's time ? *O can you think* I will ?

" By Heaven, my *soul* is yours, and tho' you kill
" Me also in your jealousy, the thrill
" Of such a death can be but ecstasy—
" No ! not for life eternal would I fly."

Elléna.

And bearing up the corpse, I hurried by,
A prey to racking thoughts, and passed the door,
And reached the street, she following with a light,
And lingering there to listen ; and I bore
My ghastly burden, favored by the night,
'Mid shading trees unnoticed, to the bank
Where darkly past the Guadalquiver flowed,
And heaving it with all my strength, it sank
With sullen splash, then all was still, nor showed
A trace, save circling eddies,—and I stood
And watched them whirling,—till methought the flood
Rose to receive me, whilst the fiends of hell
With mocking laughter shouted, and the strife
And war of waters deafened, and I fell,
Losing all sense of memory and life."

*　　*　　*　　*　　*　　*

He ceased!—the fire-glow flickered on his face,
The night-wind sighed in unison with grief.
The faults, the frailties of the human race,
Our love, our hopefulness, and fond belief,
All passed before us ; and the hollow words
Of cold philosophy, in death relief,
Seemed almost truthful, as they struck the chords

Elléna.

Of hidden recollections, and they swept
Across our fancy, while the frozen tears
Came welling up, unbidden, as unwept!
And yet we only fancied so—for years
Had clothed him in the careless masque of mien,
That ofttimes hides the tortured heart, and gives
An air of happiness, while secret pain
With vampire hunger drains the hope that lives
A ghostlike wanderer 'mid ruined hopes—
A dreary wilderness the world we tread—
No ray of sunlight where death's portal opes—
More dead than living, *buried yet not dead.*

A FRAGMENT.

'TWAS in the summer-time, and every flower,
All loving languor, sighed her soul away
In subtle fragrance,—while the wanton showers
Still lingering kissed them, loverlike, and came
   To snatch another and another kiss.
'Twas nearly evening, and the crimsoning rays
Of amber-satined sunset stole between
The close-drawn curtains that shut out the day,
Veiléd to twilight in the hushed boudoir,
In the sweet summer-time of soft July.
And waiting in expectancy I dreamed—

A Fragment.

And love enthrallèd listened, wild with hope,
While all the twittering voices of the trees
Chirrupped their happiness so musically,
The silver melody came floating in
As boyhood's dream-songs *only* dreamed and lost.
But soon the rustling of a dress, and then—
A hand of silken-smoothness clasped with mine,
And tingling sent a torrent thro' my veins,
Resistless, leaping onward, past control
Of common friendship and its usages,
And every thought of her was whelmed in one—
One maddening wish to tell her everything.
And yet I dared not,—lest in disbelief
Of all sincerity and her own sweet self,
The cruel fancy that I wooed for gold
Should rise forbidding, and appearances
But serve to strengthen it, till I became
A mere adventurer—a fortune hunter;
A wild, conceited spendthrift in her eyes.
And so we talked of everything but love;—
On many subjects, of the wond'rous sights
Seen in strange countries, and from this to that,
On to religion and her Convent life;

A Fragment.

Till all at once we puzzled for a name—
She had forgot the English, I the French ;
I guessed a lamp, but no 'twas not the word
But something like it, and she laughing rose—
A queen in height and gesture, and swept by
And sought for what she meant and brought it to me—
A handsome *cierge*, a present she received,—
One of the many for her chapel, given
By friends and relatives in pious zeal,
And love of her and heaven intertwined.
So chatting on, she graceful led the way
Toward the chapel, and I followed her—
Till passing by a tiny door she paused,
Turning her dark unfathomable eyes,
All langorous, enquiringly on mine
And opened it ; with " Look, how like you it?
" T'is rather small ! t'was fashioned for a cell,
"What think you? t'is intended for the Priest."
Then *all* I wished I know not : but I know
Curst jealousy unreasoning held me dumb.
I envied him, the holy man of God—
And instant, impious longing thrilled me through.
I wished myself a Priest to live with her,

A Fragment.

Idolatrously happy; and conceived
Her gentle voice, all tremulously soft,
By memory swept, like harp-strings with the wind,
Sobbing confession of her maiden sins.

AU REVOIR.

THE memories of parting shall encounter the anticipations of meeting,
And the tears of the one shall be mingled with the tears of the other,
And they shall form, as it were, a necklace round the neck of desire,
Till, peradventure, the sun of hope shall shine upon them,
And the rainbow of promise shall span the river of separation.

NOTES.

NOTES.

ZEBŪNĪSA.

1.—A large and celebrated garden in Upper India, consisting of tiers of marble terraces and fountains, and abounding with the most enchanting fruit trees and flowers. It was a favorite resort of Royalty, and still bears ample testimony to the taste, magnificence and luxury of the ancient rulers of the land.

2.—Many of the rich, native ladies wear belts of silver. They are worn very loose so as to hang down in front from the weight of the clasp, which is usually very massive and often engraved with some verse or sentence.

3.—The oriental plane, a magnificent tree, and deservedly a great favourite.

4.—A long, loose, thick white cotton gown, worn more especially by the Mussulman women when they go out to bathe or to take the air; it reaches from the head, which it covers together with the face, to below the ankles. It is gathered in by plaits round the neck only, and even the holes for the eyes and mouth are covered over with fine network, so that it forms the most impenetrable of disguises.

5.—Loose drawers, secured round the waist by a running silk string of many colors, with long gold or silver lace tassels.

6.—Bracelets; they are often worn above as well as below the elbow.

7.—Anklets made of silver, having little silver balls in them, about the size of a pea, so that they ring and jingle as the wearer walks.

8.—The Eastern beauties stain the palms of their hands and the soles of their feet a deep pink, with henna.

9.—A small looking-glass, called Arsi, usually very handsomely set in gold and precious stones. It is worn on the thumb as a ring.

10.—A carriage drawn by bullocks, being a sort of tent with dome-shaped top, on wheels. The tent is generally of red cloth, and its purdahs, or curtains,

Notes.

are fringed with rows of small bells. Some of the bullocks are very fine animals, the Nagauri are held in the highest esteem; they are generally pure white, can trot as fast as an ordinary horse, and cost £40 or £50 sterling apiece.

11.—A native of Kashmir. The women, more especially those of the higher ranks, may be classed among the loveliest of their sex; they are tall and well formed with gazelle eyes, perfect features, and a skin and complexion to be envied by the the fairest of European *belles*.

12.—A high native functionary connected with the Law Courts. His is an office perhaps far more lucrative than honorable, as he often receives bribes from both plaintiff and defendant.

13.—The more correct rendering of Shalabargh, the latter being a corruption of Shalimarbargh. There are several gardens of this name in India, the most famous being those overlooking the Lake, near Srinnuger (the capital of Kashmir.)

14.—The principal cities of India are walled round, and have many gates, all more or less imposing, some of them of great architectural beauty.

15.—The walls of many of the houses are covered with paintings of men, animals, flowers, &c.

16.—All the houses of the rich have a small door in them, so placed as to be scarcely noticed by a stranger or casual observer: this entrance is used by the ladies of the establishment, and by their visitors and servants only.

17.—A lady's name, signifying "heart-stealer."

18.—Common terms of respect, as are also "Benefactress of the Poor," "Queen of Sunshine," &c., &c.

19.—An Eastern proverb, a true one all over the world.

20.—Mirrors: The walls and ceilings of the rooms in the houses of the wealthy, are often adorned very gorgeously with gilding, painting of various colors and design, and a profusion of very small mirrors.

21.—The translation of the name Zebunisa.

22.—Silvery bosom: Silver-bodied, a favorite image of the oriental poets.

23.—A curved sword. The scimitar of India.

24.—In the house, the ladies wear a very fine description of colored doputah, (long veil, or mantilla) of silk-gauze, edged and flowered with gold. Some of them are very expensive; the best are manufactured at Benares.

Notes.

25.—Golden sun: Called a Chouk; it is a flat gold ornament, usually in the shape of a sun and set with jewels: it is worn on the back of the head on a plait of hair mixed with silk and gold thread, the stars are worn round the sun, attached to it by silk strings.

26.—They are like the most perfect white roses in miniature, and emit an exquisite and delicious perfume, more especially when crushed. The native women string them into necklaces and bracelets, and also strew them on their couches.

27.—A box filled with many bottles containing different kinds of scents and essences.

28.—A box, usually of gold or silver, containing betel-nut and spices, etc.

29.—A wadded quilt, which serves either as quilt or mattress.

30.—A kind of stays, fitting closely, enclosing the breasts only, made of velvet, silk, or silk gauze, and often very handsomely embroidered with gold and seed pearls, and even with jewels.

UP IN THE HILLS.

31.—A kind of palanquin. It is borne by four bearers (usually natives of Kashmir), dressed in fancy livery, according to the taste of the fair occupant, and seldom understanding a word of English and but very little Hindostanee, so that they are necessarily most discreet.

EVELEEN.

32.—A foreigner,—the term applied to Europeans.

33.—A light, native drum, usually beaten on by the fingers.

34.—A kind of lute, with wire strings. The instrument *par excellence* of India.

35.—An intoxicating potion, made from hemp.

36.—Dancing girls.

37.—It is related that on the arrival of the detachment of the 78th Highlanders at Cawnpore, after the massacre, they by some means or other, found and identified the remains of one of General Wheeler's daughters. The sight was horrible, and aroused them to such a pitch of ferocity that, gathering around, they cut off the hair from the poor girl's head, part of which was carefully selected and sent home

Notes.

to her surviving friends. The remainder they divided equally amongst themselves, and on each man receiving his carefully served out portion, they all very quietly applied themselves to the tedious task of counting the number of hairs in each individual's lot; and when this task was accomplished, they one and all swore most solemnly that for as many hairs as they held in their fingers so many of the cowardly and treacherous mutineers should die by their hands.

ELLENA.

39.—The minal-pheasants. They are rather large birds, with a plumage of the brightest shades that can possibly be imagined, of gold, golden-green, purple, black and orange. Very difficult to get at, and rarely met with except on the highest ranges of the snow-capped mountains, where darting down from their summits, with the sunlight gleaming on their outspread wings, they throw a light over the snow, composed of all the varied tints of the rainbow. The Kashmiris generally cover their heads, faces, and shoulders with a white cotton cloth when stalking them.

40.—Ibex. A large species of goat, remarkable for having long recurved horns. Many sportsmen return yearly to Kashmir solely for the Ibex shooting, and leaving Srinnuger and all the delights of the happy valley behind them, start off with their chikaris (native hunters) for the mountains.

41.—The Pir-Punjal, or mid Hymalaya range, crossed on the March to Kashmi *via* Bhimbur.

42.—The most lovely lotus, white, yellow, and pale pink, grow in the lake.

43.—This delightful tree attains great luxuriance in Kashmir, its bole is of a fine, white, smooth bark, and its foliage, of a bright green, forms a glittering and compact tuft at the summit.

44.—The Naseem-bargh. A large park-like garden, planted with alleys of magnificent chenar trees on the opposite side of the lake to, and exactly facing the world-famed Shalimar gardens of Kashmir.

45.—The custom of drowning fair ladies in sacks was much in vogue here at one time, and it is asserted that even at the present day the practice is not altogether obsolete.

46. Sim-badan. Silver-bodied; with a body fair as silver. See notes 11 and 22 page 96.

47.—The Feast of Roses. The scene presented during the first days of the Festival, is of the most animated and enchanting. Hundreds of boats crowded with gaily attired people, flinging handfuls of the most fragrant roses at each other; the

Notes.

soft tinkling of zitars, often accompanied by the sweet voices of women. The glorious summer sunshine, or fairer still, the moon mirrored in the waters of the Lake, as in a sea of molten silver; the plash of paddles mingling with the hum of merriment as the boatmen sweep onwards through the lotus-lilies, even apart from the many associations conjured up by history and romance, go to form a picture of dreamland, never altogether forgotten or effaced.

48.—The ruins of the Peri-Mahal (or abode of the Fairies) are still seen from the lake. It was in this palace, filled with the loveliest women, and surrounded by every conceivable and inconceivable luxury, that the Mogul Emperors anticipated the joys of the Mahommedan paradise, and revelled to excess in all the manifold pleasures promised to true believers.

49.—Wild he-goat. Markor is a Persian word, signifying " snake-eater."

50.—The monarch of Indian stags, having twelve points on his antlers. Barah means " twelve," and Singh is a title of honor.

51.—Chikor. The Bartavelle or Greek partridge, (*Perdix rufa,*) said to be enamoured of the moon, and to eat fire at the full moon.

www.ingramcontent.com/pod-product-compliance
Lightning Source LLC
Chambersburg PA
CBHW021948160426
43195CB00011B/1270